TOBY LURIE

POETRY CONVERSATIONS FOR TWO, THREE, AND FOUR VOICES

MIRROR
IMAGES

CELESTIAL ARTS
Millbrae, California

*"Two Poems on Parting" (Voice 2) appeared
in New Forms New Spaces, San Francisco:
Journeys into Language, 1971.*

*"Changes" appeared in New Forms New
Spaces, San Francisco: Journeys into
Language, 1971.*

*"Color Improvisations No. 3" appeared in
A Handbook on Vocal Poetry, San Francisco:
Journeys into Language, 1974.*

First Printing, August 1974
Library of Congress Card No.: 74-9758
ISBN: 0-912310-79-0
Made in the United States of America

FOREWORD

With enthusiasm and nostalgia, nine months later my students in Berkeley are still writing me about it. Why, they ask, isn't 'life' always 'like that' ?

The object of their affectionate remembrance was a session with Toby Lurie, in a rather gloomy room in Wheeler Hall. I had opened the lecture-room windows for a melioristic whiff of magnolias which bedazzle the campus, but the class's spirits were not at first conspicuously high. "Some crazy hippy poet," they seemed to be muttering, "when what we need is Milton, Spenser, and Wordsworth." I was reminded, disconcertingly, of Yeats's poem *"On Hearing that the Students of our New University Have Joined the Agitation Against Immoral Literature.* So I quickly, almost diffidently, introduced Toby to them, threw him to the lions, and prayed for some divine supervention.

My prayer, I believe, was heard by none other than Apollo.
Within minutes, hitherto lethargic or indifferent students were
sitting up and taking notice: the quality of their listening
changed, became tense and expectant, almost collaborative,
and before the session was over they had performed actions
they had never suspected themselves to be capable of; they
had improvised and interacted, they had refined their aware-
ness of palatalization, of labials and dentals, they had made
extraordinary mouth-music, and they had delighted un-
affectedly in the subtler pleasures of vocalising.

Analysis, if you like, had been supplanted by synthesis; the
exclusively cerebral, by the whole organism, including, I
hasten to add, the mind; passive recipients had become active
participants. In sum, they had been re-animated, socially,
pedagogically, poetically, and intellectually.

"If only," I heard someone murmur, "if only everybody
could have such experiences." In the best of possible worlds,
they could; but as things are, most of us will have to make do
with Toby Lurie's books and with his record. But the crucial
elements in that transforming session — namely, active partic-
ipation, alertly attentive collaboration — these are equally
important in *your* response to these poems.

Read them *aloud*, with one or two friends. If you have no
friends, go out and apprehend some unsuspecting passers-by.
I'm confident that, when they are all through with the book,
they will thank you for having buttonholed them.

Some readers are puzzled and disconcerted, at least initially,
by Toby Lurie's poetry; yet anyone familiar with the recent
history of art, music, and literature will have little difficulty
in recognizing that this poetry belongs in the contemporary
mainstream. It is neither bizarre nor eccentric but rather the

kind of poetry that we might legitimately expect from a
generously talented poet who is continuously attentive and
responsive to music, the speaking voice, social interactions,
Dadaist aesthetics, the work of Cage and Foss, improvisatory
theater, transactionalist psychology, and artistic aleatorism.
But far from being a promiscuous potpourri, the poetry bears
the unmistakable marks of a particular, individual, sensibility.
And as for my remarks on technical and stylistic influences
and trends, Toby might well remind me of Sir Edward Elgar's
remark to a friend after hearing a performance of his own
great oratorio, *The Dream of Gerontius:* "Billy, I believe there
is a lot of stuff called double counterpoint, or whatever they
call it, in that."

There is, indeed, a lot of stuff called double counterpoint,
not to mention mirror images and silence and syncopation,
etc., etc., in these poems. But let's leave the next generation
of doctoral candidates to tease their minds over such matters.
Our pleasure as readers/performers, is to delight in the ex-
perience of reenactment and realization, and in so doing to
speak both with ourselves and to others. And that, I suspect,
is exactly what Toby Lurie would like.

Geoffrey Summerfield
York, England

PRELUDE

Here are poems
and feelings
laced together
for several voices.

They must be read aloud
to become fully alive.

Some are fugues
or mirror-images.
In this form
the same words are spoken
by each voice
to create dialogue
and alter meanings
through shifted relationships.

Some of these works
combine several poems.
It is exciting to discover
how unrelated texts
can suddenly engage
in meaningful conversation.

Other poems in this book
have been created by the use
of chance or random techniques:
by dropping words in space,
picking words from a container,
or throwing coins or sticks
to determine relationships.

I believe strongly
in the validity and beauty
of chance discoveries.

In reading these poems
the space between words
should be treated as silence.
This is most important
as it allows for the interchange
between voices.

In themselves
these poems are not final,
but a step in the direction
of spontaneous interaction
between people.

The next step would be
for several people to pick
books at random
open any page
and start reading.
But each must listen
to the other and be influenced
by what he hears.

And the final step
is to come together
with others
to express deep feelings
without need for the
written word.

When this happens,
man's perfect poems will be born.

CONTENTS

PREFACE

```
1    This is a book              of poetry              to be read
2                  This is                    a book
3                          This


1
2    of poetry                          to be read
3              is a book of poetry              to be read


1    ALOUD                        by several voices. It gives to
2              ALOUD              by several voices.
3                      ALOUD   by several voices.


1    language          the added dimemsions
2              It gives                    to language
3                                              It gives


1                              of sound
2    the added dimensions              of sound
3                      to language


1    and dialogue.
2              and dialogue.
3                              the added dimensions of sound


1                  But for it to work each person must be willing
2
3    and dialogue.


1              to shed
2    For it to work          each person
3                              For it to work
```

```
1                                                    a bit of ego
2    must be willing              to shed
3                        each person


1                    to listen                    and be touched.
2                          to listen
3    must be willing                    to listen


1                         Then he will be influenced
2    be touched.                                    Then
3              touched.


1    by what he hears                          and his words
2                    he will be influenced
3                                        Then


1                    will come alive.
2    by what he hears
3                                        he will be influenced


1
2    and his words                    will come alive.
3                    by what he hears.


1    Some of these poems        are free fugues
2                        Some                    of these poems
3


1    or imitations
2                    are free fugues
3                                Some of these poems
```

1   others are shattered and
2   *or imitations*
3   are free fugues

1   reassembled   in a way
2   *others are*   *shattered*
3   or imitations

1   not unlike Cubism
2   *and reassembled*
3   others are   shattered

1   or Dadaism.
2   *in a way*   *not unlike Cubism*
3   and reassembled

1   But are they poems?   What is a poem?
2   *or Dadaism.*
3   in a way

1
2   *But are they poems?*
3   not unlike Cubism   or Dadaism.

1   Who may decide?
2   *What a poem is?*
3   But are they poems?

1   Is a poet a poem?   Is a poem a poet?
2   *Who may decide?*
3

1   I call myself a poet
2   *Is a poet a poem?*
3 What is a poem?

1   It makes me feel good
2   *Is a poem a poet?*
3 Who may decide?

1   but I don't know
2   *I call myself a poet*
3 Is a poet a poem?

1   what it means
2   *it makes me feel good*
3 Is a poem a poet?

1   and I don't really care.
2   *what it means*
3 I call myself a poet

1   I just want to succeed
2
3 it makes me feel good

1
2 *I don't really care.*   *I just want to succeed*
3   but I don't know

1 in creating excitement   and energy
2
3   I don't really care.

1
2   *in creating excitement*
3   I just want to succeed

1   and feelings
2   *and energy*
3   in creating excitement

1   with language.
2   *and feelings*
3   and energy   and feelings

1
2   *with language.*
3   with language.

MIRROR IMAGES
AND
FUGUES

From the beginning, Dada was thus replaced by a
thoroughly blurred mirror image of itself. Since then
even the mirror has broken. Anyone who finds a frag-
ment of it can now read into it his own image of Dada,
conditioned by his own aesthetic, national, historical
or personal beliefs and preferences.

Hans Richter
Dada: Art and Anti-Art

THE MOMENT

```
1   The moment of being is so fragile.            It is all
2                                         The moment
3

1                                                that we have
2   of being               is so fragile.
3          The moment                      of being

1           for the moment beyond          the moment
2   It is all
3                                     is so fragile.

1              in which we exist
2   that we have                        for the moment
3                            It is all

1   is the eternity
2              beyond              the moment
3                    that we have

1   which will never come                  to us.
2
3                          for the moment

1                                        It is
2   in which we exist        is the eternity
3               beyond                  the moment

1                    in this moment
2   which will never come
3                            in which we exist
```

2

1   that we are born
2   *to us.*   *It is*
3   is the eternity   which will never

1   and that we die.
2   *in this moment*
3   come to us.   It is

1   And sadly
2   *that we are born*   *and that we die.*
3   in this moment

1   it is   in this moment
2   *And sadly*
3   that we are   born

1   that many of us
2   *it is in this moment*
3   and that   we die.

1   barely exist   caught as we are
2
3   And sadly it is

1
2   *that many of us*   *barely exist*
3   in this moment

1   in the anxiety of moments
2   *caught*
3   that many of us barely exist

1   past or future.
2   *as we are*   *in the anxiety*
3   caught   as we are

2   *of moments*   *past or future.*
3   in the anxiety

3   of moments past or future.

WORD

1   To open it in a gentle surgery.
2   *To open it*

1   To send it   soaring
2   *in a gentle*   *surgery.*

1   on the waves of sound.   To release it
2   *To send it*

1   from itself,
2   *soaring*   *on the waves of*

1   sound and rhythm   its accomplices
2   *sound.*

1   (mulched   in a tender throat).
2   *To release it*   *from itself,*

1   Words become
2   *sound and*   *rhythm its accomplices*

1   what they say.
2   *(mulched in a tender throat).*

1   Words become   their reality.
2   *Words become*

1
2   *what they say.*

TRIO

1 This is a poem for three voices
2   *This is a poem*
3

1 that asks each voice   to listen
2   *for three voices*
3

1   to create silence
2   *that asks each voice*
3 This is a poem

1
2   *to listen*
3 for three voices   that asks each voice

1 and to feel.
2   *to create silence*
3   to listen

1 That shows by doing
2   *and to feel.*
3   to create silence

1 that poems   can be read
2   *That shows*   *by doing*
3

1 together   to enhance meaning.
2
3   and to feel.   That shows

1   This is a poem
2   *that poems*   *can be read together*
3   by doing

1   that become three poems
2   *to enhance meaning.*
3   that poems

1
2   when given to
2   *This is a poem*
3   can be read   together

1   three voices
2
3   *that becomes three poems*
3   to enhance meaning.

1   each voice bringing   its quality
2
3   This is   a poem

1   into the whole   and adding
2   *when given*   *to three voices*
3

1   to poetry
2   *each voice*
3   that becomes   three poems

1   the dimension
2   *bringing its*
3   when given to three voices

1   of dialogue.
2   *quality*   *into the whole*
3   each voice

1   This is a poem   that says
2   *and adding*
3   bringing its quality

1   we
2   *to poetry*   *the dimension*   *of dialogue.*
3   into the whole

1   should come together
2
3   and adding to poetry

1   celebrate together
2   *This is a poem*
3   the dimension

1   create together
2   *that says*
3   of dialogue.   This is a poem

1   and understand
2   *we should come together*
3   that says

1   together.
2   *celebrate together*
3   we should come together

1   This is a poem
2   *create together*
3   celebrate together

1   a simple poem
2   *and understand together.*
3   create together

1   which I hope
2   *This is a poem*
3   and understand together.

1   succeeds in expressing
2   *a simple poem*
3   This is a poem

1   the idea
2   *which I hope*   *succeeds in expressing*
3   a simple poem

1   that the human voice   is an instrument
2   *the idea*
3   which I hope

1
2   *that the human voice*
3   succeeds in expressing the idea

1   of infinite possibilities.
2   *is an instrument*
3   that the human voice

1   is an instrument of infinite possibilities.
2   *of infinite possibilities. is an instrument of infinite possibilities.*
3   is an instrument of infinite possibilities.

REFLECTIONS

1 Echoing moonlight
2   *Echoing moonlight*

1 colder than my hair.
2   *colder than my hair.*

1 Weeping time in the washroom.
2   *Weeping time in the washroom.*

1 The year shudders. Poems cease.
2   *The year shudders.*

1 Calligraphy on tangled cliff   silent as seaweed
2 *Poems cease.*

1   Drifting mountain
2 *Calligraphy on tangled cliff silent as seaweed.*

1   green world. The stillness
2 *Drifting mountain   green world.*   *The stillness*

1 the void.   Contemplate spring   water clear
2   *the void.*   *Contemplate spring*

1   mountain creek silent white.
2 *water clear*   *mountain creek silent white.*

1   [silence.] Holy cold moonlight exceeds spirit.
2   *Holy cold moonlight exceeds spirit.*

1   Rock poems cease.
2   *Rock poems cease.*

1   Cliff poems cease.
2   *Cliff poems cease.*

1   Troubles from a cold mind.
2   *Troubles from a cold mind.*

THAT WHICH

1   That which is is that which is   that,
2   *That which is*

1   and that   which isn't isn't
2   *is that*   *which is that,*

1   that which wasn't   unless
2   *and*   *that which isn't*

1   that which isn't   wasn't ever
2   *isn't*   *that which wasn't*

1   was.   For that which isn't
2   *unless*   *that*   *which isn't,*

1   that   but was   that is that
2   *wasn't ever was.*   *For that*

1   which was
2   *which isn't that*   *but was that*

1   and that which   wasn't that
2   *is that*   *which was*

1   but is that   is that
2   *and that*   *which wasn't that*

1   which is.
2   *is that which was.*

MIRROR IMAGES

1 Summer madness, shadows dancing
2   Summer madness,

1 on sunbaked walls   in silent calligraphy.
2   shadows dancing

1   Children's voices
2 on sunbaked walls   in silent calligraphy.

1 mingled   with seaweed   and surf
2   Children's voices   mingled

1   roar.   At midnight   silence
2 with seaweed   and surf   roar.

1   as earth   cools.
2 At midnight   silence   as earth cools.

IN CASE OF EMERGENCY

1   Know how to move out of the plane
2   *Know how to move*

1   fast.   If such should occur
2   *out of the plane*

1   over 500 feet
2   *fast.*
3   Know how to move   out

1   above landing surface,
2   *If such should occur*
3

1   know how to fly.
2   *over 500 feet*
3   of the plane

1   There is fire danger
2   *above landing surface,*
3   fast.

1
2   *know how to fly.*
3   If such should occur   Over 500 feet

1   anytime a landing is other
2
3   above landing surface,

1 than normal
2 *There is fire danger*
3 know how to fly.

1 but normal landings are a rarity.
2 *anytime* *a landing*
3

1 Below is a floor plan
2 *is other than normal*
3

1
2 *but normal landings are a rarity.*
3 There is fire danger

1 of the plane you are in.
2
3 anytime a landing is other

1 Memorize it
2 *Below is a floor plan*
3 than normal

1
2 *of the plane*
3 but normal landings are a rarity.

1 so that in the event
2
3 Below is a floor plan

1 of sudden fire   or explosion
2   *you are in.*   *Memorize it*
3

1 you can   calmly and efficiently
2   *so that*
3   of the plane

1   find the nearest exit
2   *in the event of sudden fire*
3 you are in.

1   if it is still there.
2   *or explosion*
3 Memorize it   so that

1 When leaving   move to the exits
2   *you can calmly*
3

1
2   *and efficiently*
3 in the event of sudden fire   or explosion

1   immediately.
2 *find the nearest exit*   *if it is still there.*
3

1 Do not go for coats, purses,
2   *When leaving*
3   you can calmly

1
2
3   body parts ,or other

  and efficiently find the nearest

1   personal items.   Line up
2   *move to the exits*   *immediately.*
3

1   and
2   *Do not go for coats, purses, body parts,*
3   exit

1   pass through the exits
2
3   if it is still there.

1
2   *or other personal items.*
3   When leaving move

1   in alphabetical order.
2   *Line up*
3   to the exits immediately.

1
2   *and pass through the exits*
3   Do not go for coats, purses,

1
2   *in alphabetical order,*
3   body parts,   or other personal items.

1   Bon Voyage . . .

THIS MOMENT

1   This moment is all that we have for in
2   *This moment is*

1   this moment is   all of life.
2   *all that we have*

1   And life is   now
2   *for in this*   *moment*   *is all*

1   and never was   before
2   *of life.*   *And life is now*

1   or after.   The moment
2   *and never*   *was before*

1   beyond   this moment
2   *or after.*   *The moment*

1   will never be felt   for though it be
2   *beyond*   *this moment*

1   an eternity   it has no   existence.
2   *will never be*   *felt*

1   We are born   in this moment
2   *for*   *though it be*

1   and we die
2   *an eternity*   *it has no existence.*

1 in this moment   and all space
2   *We are born*

1   between   is enclosed
2 *in this moment*   *and we die*

1   within   this moment.
2 *in this moment*   *and all space*

1   That moment   which exists beyond
2 *between*   *is enclosed*

1   this moment   can only be felt
2 *within*   *this moment.*

1   as this moment
2 *That moment*   *which exists*

1 which is its only existence.
2   *beyond this moment*

1 Beyond   and before
2 *can only be felt*   *as this moment*

1 are fantasy.
2 *which is its only existence.*

FUGHETTA

```
1    Slanting bars of silver                    strung
2                        Slanting bars
3                                               Slanting


1                    from morning
2    of silver                      strung
3              bars                      of silver


1    glory                 to black metal
2          from morning
3                                   strung from


1                    shuddering
2    glory                        to black
3          morning                     glory


1    in               a wind.
2        metal                shuddering
3            to black                  metal


1
2    in a            wind.
3        shuddering       in a wind.
```

20

CHANGES

1   There was a mountain over there. I saw it
2

                                   clearly
1
2   *There was a mountain*   *over there.*

1   last year   or was it
2   *I saw it*   *clearly*

1   the year before   or the year before.
2   *last year*

1   And the sun
2   *or was it*   *the year before*

1   has turned to blood.
2   *or the year before.*

1   There was a sea   over there
2   *And the sun*

1   I remember it.
2   *has turned to blood.*   *There was a sea*

1   The colors blue, green,   emerald,
2   *over there*

1   sparkling orange   from the moon.
2   *I remember it.*

21

1   My body became
2   *The colors blue, green,*   *emerald,*

1   wet in that sea,
2   *sparkling orange from the moon.*

1   deliciously cold.   I can hear you
2   *My body*   *became wet*

1   but I cannot see   you sea.
2   *in that sea,*

1   I saw you
2   *deliciously cold.*   *I can hear you*

1   clearly last year
2   *but I cannot see you sea.*

1   or was it the year before   or the year before?
2   *I saw you*

1   And the sun   has turned
2   *clearly*   *last year*   *or was it*

1   to blood.   And there was a forest.
2   *the year before*

1   I remember you
2   *or the year before?*   *And the sun*

1 forest.   Heavy,   thick with colors
2   *has turned*   *to blood.*

1   and trees
2 *And there was a forest.*   *I remember you forest.*

1 and streams   and sweet   smells.
2   *Heavy,*   *thick*

1   I walked in you forest
2 *with colors and trees*

1   Slept inside   of you.
2 *and streams*   *and sweet smells.*

1   My head and lungs
2 *I walked*   *in you forest.*

1 were full of you.   But where
2   *Slept*   *inside of you.*

1 are you now?   What has become
2   *My head*

1   of you?
2 *and lungs were full of you.*   *But*

1 I saw you clearly   last year
2   *where are you now?*

1   or was it   the year before
2   *What has become*   *of you?*

1   or the year before?
2   *I saw you*   *clearly last year*

1   And the sun   has turned to blood
2   *or was it*

1   the sun   has turned
2   *the year before*   *or the year*

1   to blood   sun has turned
2   *before?*   *And the sun*

1   to blood   has turned   to blood
2   *has turned*   *to blood*

1   turned to blood   to blood
2   *the sun has turned*   *to blood*

1   to blood   blood.
2   *has turned*   *to blood.*

SYMBOLS

1   Pen scratching on paper, symbols flopping
2

1   symbolic   of flopping symbols.
2   *Pen scratching*   *on paper,*

1   What is there
2   *symbols flopping*   *symbolic of*

1   past experience   but a memory?
2   *flopping symbols.*

1   What do we record
2   *What is there*   *past experience*

1   but a symbol   of that memory?
2   *but a memory?*

1   What is there
2   *What do we record*   *but a symbol*

1   before experience   but a suppose or
2   *of that memory?*

1   maybe?
2   *What is there*   *before experience*

1   What do we record   but a symbol
2   *but a suppose*

1   of that suppose
2 or maybe?   *What do we record*

1 or maybe?   What do we receive
2   but a symbol of

1   but a symbol of that memory
2 that suppose or maybe?

1   or suppose or maybe
2 What do we receive

1   measuring symbols
2 but a symbol   *of that memory*

1 with symbols   splitting
2   or suppose or maybe

1   augmenting.
2 measuring   *symbols with symbols*

1 What do we understand?   What we feel.
2   splitting

1   What do we feel?
2 augmenting.   *What do we understand?*

1 What we understand.   What has become
2   What we feel.

1   of the experience?
2   *What do we feel?*   *What we understand.*

1   What has become
2   *What has become*   of the memory?

1   What has become
2   *of the experience?*   *What has become*

1   of the suppose   or maybe?
2   *of the memory?*

1   Pen scratching on paper,
2   *What has become of the*

1   symbols flopping
2   *suppose or maybe?*   *Pen scratching*

1   flopping symbols,   flopping symbols,
2   *on paper,*

1   flopping symbols.
2   *symbols flopping*   *flopping symbols.*

WHAT IS SAD

1   What is sad really very sad at least to me it's sad

1   so very sad
2   *What is sad*   *really very sad*

1   is the whithering   that comes
2   *at least to me*

1   in middle age.   It comes
2   *it's sad*   *so very sad*

1   (we see it)   of the soul
2   *is the withering*   *that comes*

1   a whithering   to the soul
2   *in middle age.*   *It comes*

1   we see it   in middle age
2   *(we see it)*   *of the soul*

1   a whithering   of the heart
2   *a whithering*   *to the soul*

1   and it is sad   so very sad
2   *we see it*   *in middle age*

1   this withering of the heart
2   *a whithering*

1   this whithering that comes   in middle age
2   *of the heart*

1   a whithering of the soul
2   *and it is sad*   *so very sad*

1   a whithering of the heart
2   *this whithering*

1   a whithering of joy   and laughter
2   *of the heart*

1   is sad
2   *this whithering that comes   in middle age*

1   so sad   that withering of the soul
2   *a whithering of*

1   that whithering of the heart
2   *the soul*   *a whithering*

1   that whithering of joy
2   *of the heart*   *a whithering*

1   and laughter   whithering of the mind
2   *of joy*   *and laughter*

1   that comes   in middle age.
2   *is sad*   *so sad*

1   How sad that whithering
2   *that whithering of the soul*

1   that comes
2   *that whithering*   *of the heart*

1   in middle age   that comes
2   *that whithering*

1   in middle age   that comes
2   *of joy*   *and laughter*

1   in middle age   that comes
2   *whithering*   *of the mind.*

1   in middle age
2   *How sad*   *that whithering that*

1   comes in   comes in
2   *middle age*   *middle age*

1   comes in   comes in
2   *middle age*   *middle age*

BEGINNINGS

1   Before man discovered words he must have had some sort of very basic language of communication.

1   It certainly wasn't
2   *Before man*   *discovered*

1   very universal.   In fact,
2   *words*   *he must have had*

1   each family unit   must have had
2   *some sort of*

1   its own special
2   *very basic*   *language of communication.*

1   language system.   I'm sure
2   *It certainly wasn't*

1   this caused great confusion
2   *very universal.*

1   as families began to move
2   *In fact,*   *each family unit*

1   about and mingle   with other families.
2   *must have had*

1   Every time
2   *its own special language system.*

1   new groups came together
2   *I'm sure*   *this caused great*

1   it must have been necessary
2   *confusion*

1   to reorganize
2   *as families began to move about*

1   language.   And as family groups
2   *and mingle*

1   became clusters
2   *with other families.*

1   and clusters
2   *Every time new groups*

1   became tribes, language
2   *came together it*   *must have*

1   became more and more   complicated.
2   *been necessary*

1   I feel, that at this point,
2   *to reorganize language.*

1   the language
2   *And as family groups*   *became clusters*

1 of words   must have been born.
2   *and clusters*

1   And while one might conclude
2 *became tribes,*

1   that the birth of language
2 *language became more*

1 was the first great   step
2 *and more*   *complicated.*

1 in the direction   of logic
2 *I feel,*   *that at this point,*

1   and understanding
2 *the language of words*

1   one might also consider
2 *must have been born.*

1   that it was responsible
2 *And while one might conclude*

1   for a great deal
2 *that the birth of language was*

1 of confusion
2 *the first great step*   *in the direction of logic.*

1 and misunderstanding.

DO

1   It is necessary that we do   what we must
2   *It is*

1   do.   To do less
2   *necessary*   *that we do*

1   is to fail.   To fail
2   *what we must*   *do.*

1   is to suffer   and in this
2   *To do less*   *is to fail.*

1   so short, so fragile   existence
2   *To fail*   *is to suffer*

1   we must do   what we must.
2   *and in this*   *so short,*

1   It is necessary,   so necessary
2   *so fragile*   *existence*

1   that we do
2   *we must do*   *what we must.*

1   what we must do.   And this is said
2   *It is necessary,*

1   with the certainty
2   *so necessary*   *that we do*

1   that what we must do   we can do.
2   *what we must do.*

1   To fail in doing what we must
2   *And this is said*

1   is to fail
2   *with the certainty*   *that what we must do*

1   in this life   and this life is all
2   *we can do.*   *To fail*

1   that we have.   Nothing more
2   *in doing*   *what we must*

1   is given.   So we can do no less
2   *is to fail*   *in this life*

1   than to do   what we must
2   *and this life*   *is all*

1   and we must do
2   *that we have.*   *Nothing more*

1   what we must   do.
2   *is given.*   *So we can do no less*

1   do   do   do
2   *than what we must*   *and we must*

1   do.
2   *what we must.*

CONVERSATIONS

THREE POEMS

1 mission lawn
2   *house glowing*
3   melon in a blue pot

1 across from nativity
2   *voices through window*
3   potatoes

1   tourists flashing
2   *mother daughter planning*
3 onions tuna

1   on old mission
2
3 wrapped in scrambled eggs

1   december sun
2 *knives chopping*
3   chocolate-chip sundae

1 baking   rose garden
2
3   marshmellow-chocolate

1   (a monument of sorts)
2 *cupboards slamming*   *breakfast*
3

1   while Mary and Joseph
2 *probably cooking*
3   topping

1   stand at attention   Jesus flown
2
3   and another fast

1   somewhere
2   *tho I can't smell it*
3   is disrupted

TIME

1   There is still   time
2   *We are a tiny*   *thread*

1   for the things   to be done
2   *in the cosmic fabric,*

1   that must be done
2   *slowly turning*   *and fading*

1   before one is done.
2   *into the void.*

TWO POEMS ON PARTING

1 When it's time it's time   when it's time
2   *Goodby*   *goodby friend*

1 you'll know.   Please   don't hang on to me
2   *lover*   *most beloved.*

1   let me go.   I don't want to go
2 *I wondered*   *as you passed by*

1   but when it's time   it's time
2 *if one of us*   *should not have said*

1   to go   to go.   It's been good
2 *goodby.*   *Goodby friend*   *lover*

1   so good   and it's been bad
2 *most beloved.*   *How short the time*

1   it had   to be bad   to be good.
2 *how quick*   *the time*   *we thought*

1   That's how we grow.   I love you so
2 *we dwelled*   *in the eye*

1   and that's why
2 *of eternity*   *but that has passed*

1 you've got to let go.   When it's time
2   *as you have passed*

1   it's time   when it's time you'll know.
2   *passed*   *in a moment*

1   Please don't hang on   to me
2   *so suddenly*   *that I*   *had no time*

1 let me go.   I don't want to go
2   *to say*   *goodby.*

1 but I don't want to stay   this way
2   *Goodby friend*   *lover*

1 and I don't   want to let you go   ˙
2   *most beloved*   *I could not*

1 but when it's time it's time   and when it's time
2   *say goodby*

1   I'll know.   We don't want to go
2   *but only watch*   *you passing*

1   we don't   want to go   but when it's time
2   *passing*   *passing*   *passing*

1   we'll know   to let go   to let go
2   *passing*   *passing*   *passing by.*

1   to let go   to let go
2   *Friend*   *lover*   *most beloved*

1   to let go.
2   *goodby.*

NOTE FROM MY WIFE

1   And she wrote me
2   *Your insides are very much on my mind*

1   and she said   and I love hers and she went on
2   *I love them*

1   and that was
2   *your insides think and feel like my kind of man*

1   nice to hear and then she said
2   *your outsides are very much*

1   in this note she left me on the hall bench saying
2   *on my mind*

1   and saying
2   *and on my insides*   *in my mind and feelings*

1   and then coming from the note she said
2   *let us make love*

1   and I am waiting for her to come home.
2   *this day or night.*

YESTERDAY, TODAY

1 Yesterday   it rained
2   *Today*   *we took Sandy*

1 and I stayed away   observing you
2   *to his perhaps*

1 from the   hills at sunset.
2   *last sunset.*

1   Today you are washed clean
2 *The sun had dropped*

1   as clean as I have seen you
2 *trailing pink*

1   this season.   Ocean receded
2 *over Santa Ynez.*   *Sandy*

1   and gentle,   revealing
2 *made friends*   *with beetles,*

1   your broad, flat belly.
2 *horse turds,*   *oak trees, weeds,*

1 Sands   crusting under a bright sun.
2   *and fence posts.*

1   I accuse you of silence
2 *He barked,*

44

1   but it's not true.
2   *winked from his good side*

1   You speak
2   *and said*   *"Let's go home*

1   in many languages
2   *no one lives forever."*

1   and I am listening more carefully.

SANTA BARBARA BEACH

1   A madman   deep
2   *I would like to say*   *something*

1   in his madness   untied
2   *to you*   *my head is*

1   tennis shoes
2   *full of*   *memories sluiced*

1   ankle deep in water
2   *over 17 years of head-rock*

1   passed me   in the sand
2   *my children*   *baptized*

1   so close   I could have reached out
2   *on your shore*

1   and touched him   or said hello
2   *my wife*   *grown brown*

1   or asked him why
2   *and beautiful*   *under your sun*

1   or told him why
2   *even you desired her*

1   his arms hung
2   *how many ceremonies of love*

1   at his sides
2   *and anguish*   *did we perform*

1   and there was a look of peace
2   *before your watch.*

1   on his face.

EAST OF EAST BEACH

1 Stench of oil in the air.
2   *Vegetarian dinner*

1 Sheets of black   breaking on shore.
2   *for a few friends*

1   Sand drenched with oil
2 *around the point*   *under the cemetery*

1 no sand crabs today   all underground.
2   *near my father.*

1   A couple of terns   wandering
2 *Row to the kelp*   *racing*

1 wondering.   A few gulls floating
2   *a deflated section*   *back*

1 on the film.   Oil platforms
2   *to shore.*   *Small fire*

1 through the smog.
2   *under departing sunset.*

1 A mournful horn   blowing a requiem.
2   *Remains of dinner*

1   We'll read about it
2   *to campers*   *at night-frisbee.*

1   in the afternoon paper.

LOVE POEMS

1 Climb on   on   on
2   *Don't*   *don't complicate*   *my heart*

1 climb on   on   disrupt the agony
2   *with words*   *and anger*

1   of my vacant mind
2   *but give me*   *your eyes*

1 vacant heart   vacant soul
2   *your touch*   *silence*

1 climb on   on
2   *and sweet deeds*   *the mulch*

1 blessed one
2   *of tenderness*

LISTEN

1   Hello, there's a thing I want to tell you.
2

1   An important
2   *Prices on the New York Stock Exchange*

1   Oh God yes
2   *swung wildly this week*   *both up and down*

1   how important a thing   that you need
2   *but with all eyes*

1   to hear.
2   *on the energy crisis*   *the market suffered*

1   That you must hear   in order
2   *its 3rd consecutive week*

1   for you and me   to survive
2   *of decline*   *in the heaviest trading*

1   this life
2   *of the year.*   *Wall Street was unable to decide*

1   and flower in it
2   *the significance of Nixon's words*

1   at least a little.   So listen
2   *however*   *and profit taking*

50

1 please listen.   And this is a big part
2   *quickly whittled back*

1   of it: to listen.
2 *most of the advance.*   *The sagging rally*

1   Because if we don't listen
2 *got its second wind*

1   to each other
2 *after Soviet leader Brezhnev said*

1   we deny each other
2 *the United States and Russia*

1   and rejection
2 *had a common desire*   *for peace*

1 which leads to isolation
2   *in the Middle East.*

1 which leads to loneliness   leads to death.
2   *That announcement*

1   Not for just you and me
2 *sent the Dow up more than 20 points*

1   but for the entire world.
2 *for the second time that day.*

1   If we are to flower
2   *On Monday, for instance*

1   we must listen
2   *the Dow skidded about 19 points*

1   to each other.
2   *amid the many unanswered questions*

1   All kinds
2   *of the current energy crisis*   *but in a matter of minutes*

1   and ages   and geographies
2   *the index of 30 blue chips*

1   must listen   to each other.
2   *had won back*   *nearly half that loss*

1   This is our only chance
2   *on news*   *the House of Representatives*

1   and we are hopelessly moving
2   *had granted approval*

1   in the wrong direction.
2   *to the trans-Alaskan pipeline.*

1   Listen   by denying
2   *There were wild upswings, too.*

1   and ignoring each other
2 *On Friday*   *investors, almost desperate*

1 we are willing each other
2   *for something to cheer about*

1 out of existence.   Loneliness
2   *sent the Dow up*   *more than*

1   and isolation   is the final room
2 *20 points*   *within minutes*

1   and we are knocking
2 *after President Nixon stated,*   *"at some time*

1 on the door.   But we have the power
2   *in the future*

1   to give each other
2 *we can see some change*   *with regard to some*

1 existence
2   *of the Arab oil-producing countries*

1 as well as take it away.
2   *in their attitude*

1 By listening to each other
2   *towards exporting to the United States*

1   and to ourselves   we can mobilize against isolation.
2   *and Europe."*

1   We can fertilize
2   *Wall Street was unable to decide*

1   the seeds of life
2   *the significance*   *of Nixon's words*

1   by giving the gift   of existence
2   *however*   *and profit taking*

1   to one another.   But we must listen
2   *whittled back*

1   before it is too late.
2   *most of the advance.*

1   We must listen
2   *Sales totaled 109,326,110 shares.*

1   with feeling
2   *The previous high for 1973*   *was 105,783,060 shares*

1   and with love   we must listen.
2   *traded this week*   *ended Sept. 21.*

1   Loneliness and isolation   is the final room
2   *The week's total*

1   and we are knocking
2 *compared with 87,111,633 shares traded*

1   on the door.   So quickly
2 *a week ago*   *and with 87,376,070*

1   quickly   listen
2 *the year earlier.*   *There is no law*   *that says*

1 listen   listen
2   *an oversold condition*   *in a bear market*

1 listen   listen   listen.
2   *cannot persist.*

GUILT GAME

1 I'd like not to play   that game,
2   *I feel guilty*   *about you*

1 please.   I'd like not to substitute
2   *feeling guilty*

1   a game   for that game,
2 *for telling me*   *that I'm trying*

1   please.
2 *to make you feel guilty*   *because you know that*

1 Games are games   and I don't like 'em
2   *I'm not guilty*

1 anymore.   I don't need 'em anymore
2   *(although I feel it)*

1   and if you need 'em
2 *of trying to make you feel guilty*

1   anymore   please
2 *and I know you wouldn't*   *feel guilty*

1 find yourself   another score.
2   *unless you were sure*

1   I'm all gamed out
2 *that I was sure*   *that you felt guilty*

1   and if this is a game   that I'm playing
2   *which I'm not*

1   now   I'm stopping.
2   *which is the reason*   *that I feel guilty.*

CONVERSATION

1	How are you?	Far out.	Slow.
2	*Good, man.*	*How are things?*	

1	Things happen	
2	*Well, don't push.*	*when they happen.*

1	I'm sort of dry.	to figure things out.
2	*Sometimes it's hard*	

1	I think I need a change of space.
2	*Don't sweat it.*

1	So what's happening?
2	*Maybe space needs a change of you.*

1	Heard any good music?
2	*Smoked any good dope lately?*

1	Maybe diet
2	*I think I should do something physical.*

1	and work with your hands
2	*Maybe I'll go back to school.*

1	you're good with leather.	
2	*I' don't know.*	*I'm feeling old.*

1	I'm feeling tired.	I'm bummed out.
2	*I'm feeling bored.*	

1   We got to get our shit together.
2   *I'm spaced.*

1   Maybe a trip
2   *Yeh, we should get our shit together.*

1   Big Sur   Mendocino
2   *High Sierras*   *Frisco*   *someplace.*

1   We'll have to talk about it.   No hurry.
2   *When?*   *Not really.*

1   Oh!   Later.
2   *Keep cool.*

THE W.G. CAPER

1   Mr. Mitchell   I'm sitting
2   *I just want to make one thing clear*

1   in the sand today   under a windy sun
2   *very clear*   *perfectly clear.*

1   feeling   clean and righteous.
2   *But I really have*   *no recollection.*

1   I saw your voice   on T.V.
2   *At that point*   *in time*

1   for the second day today.
2   *weren't you sort of curious?*

1   Mr. Mitchell   I was looking
2   *I'm not here*   *as a sinner*

1   for a tear
2   *seeking a confessional.*   *with specificity*

1   so we could cry   together.
2   *in that particular time frame.*

1   I needed to cry   with you.
2   *I'd be inclined*   *to think so*

1   I wanted to take my·T.V.
2   *but I'm not certain.*

1   with you inside
2   *There was a new concern*   *and I had become*

1   in my arms   and give you comfort
2   *that concern.*

1   and brush away
2   *We have a great deal*   *to be thankful for*

1   that look.   Mr. Mitchell
2   *as Americans tonight.*   *In retrospect*

1   I looked hard   for a tear.
2   *I strongly believe*

1   Wicker said
2   *that the truth will out.*

1   "are you stone-walling it?"
2   *I have no recollection.*

1   You didn't understand
2   *When the going gets tough*

1   laced tightly
2   *the tough get going.*   *It's a damnable palpable lie.*

1   in your mask   of innocence.
2   *I was motivated*   *soley by concern*

1 I heard your voice   tremble.
2   *for the campaign.*   *And it goes on*

1 I saw your hand   tremble.   Mr. Mitchell
2   *and on*   *and on.*

1   looking at you today
2 *I want to make one thing clear*

1   I wondered
2 *perfectly clear.*   *I have no knowledge.*

1 if you really existed   and how you felt
2   *I kind of remember it*

1   inside.
2 *but not enough*   *to testify that I did.*

1 I wanted to take you   by the hand
2   *Give me*

1   along some quiet stream
2 *the thrust*   *of the conversation.*

1 and cut you open   gently
2   *Today in America*

1   and let you drain.
2 *we have a magnificent opportunity.*

1   Then I would sew you
2   *As I said*   *it's inch by inch*

1   back together   with the stems
2   *that the truth*

1   of wild flowers.
2   *is coming out.*

I AM ON THE THRESHOLD

1	I am on the threshold of the moment
2	*And it goes on*

1	of birth of the moment
2	*and it goes on* *and on* *and on*

1	of sight of the moment of touch
2	*it goes on* *it goes*

1	of the moment of the first tear.
2	*on it goes* *it goes* *on it goes*

1	The moment of laughter the moment
2	*and on* *it goes* *and on*

1	of embarrassment the moment of anger
2	*it goes* *on* *and on*

1	the moment of the first love. Moment
2	*on.* *Why must it*

1	of rejection moment of success
2	*go on* *why* *why must it go*

1	moment of failure moment
2	*must it* *go it must* *it must.*

1   of the first disaster.   Of frustration
2   *Go on*   *and it goes on*

1   of crisis   of marriage
2   *and it goes on*   *on beyond*

1   of the first child.   Moment   of divorce
2   *beyond on*   *it must go*

1
2   *beyond*   moment   of loneliness
      beyond on   *it goes beyond*

1   moment   of peace   moment of first illness.
2   *on it goes*   *it goes*

1   The moment   of truth
2   *and it goes on.*   *Do you feel it*

1   the moment   of anxiety
2   *going on*   *going on going on*

1   the moment   of longing
2   *do you feel it*   *do you feel it*

1   the moment   of the first falling.
2   *going on*   *and on*   *beyond.*

1   Of the moment   of hopelessness   of the moment
2   *Why*   *must it*

```
1          of senility        of the moment            of death
2    must it          go on                  and on
```

```
1          of the moment                    of the first returning.
2    and on                  and it goes on
```

```
1                    I am on the threshold
2    and it goes on.                        It goes
```

```
1    of every moment          every moment      every moment
2                      it goes              on
```

```
1            every moment          every moment
2    going on              it goes on              beyond
```

```
1    every moment          every moment
2              beyond                beyond
```

```
1    every moment.
2              beyond on.
```

SOUND POEMS

My Sound Poems are experiments with the colors, dynamics, energies, and rhythms which exist as the components of sound. These nonverbal poems uncover special feelings which defy definition. The exchange among the voices creates a dialogue more personal and direct then much of what happens between us in daily conversation. Here, within the *Sound Poem,* is a safe environment for releasing all the emotions which reside within our beings.

Where there is a line above the letters, the sound is sustained. Where there are dots, the sound is sharp and stacatto-like. Two lines diverging and returning together mean, from soft to loud and back to soft. And the spaces between the letters are treated as silence. Voice 1 can establish the tempo for all parts by moving his finger across the page at a constant speed. And treat the letters as sounds rather than labels. I like to think of each letter as a tube of color. When the top is re-moved it can flow and mix with the other colors to create the sound palette. Every encounter with these poems will be a new experience, for each person who comes to them will see, feel, taste, and hear them in a very personal way.

COLOR IMPROVISATION No. 3

1   r̄r̄r̄r̄r̄r̄r̄dẗ   dẗ   dẗ   r̄r̄r̄r̄r̄r̄r̄r̄dẗ   dẗ

2   sshhhhllllllllllllllllll

3   v̈b   v̈b

1   v̈d̈tooooooop   v̈d̈tooooooooop   ṗoooooooo

2   j̈k̄l̄l̄   j̈k̄l̄l̄   j̈k   j̈k   j̈k j̈k

3   sssssssssssssssẗ ẗẗsssssssssssssmmmmmmmmmmmmm

1   ṗoooooooo   poooooooooooooemmmm

2   ẅ ẅ ẅ ẅ ẅ ẅ ẅ ẅ

3   bmbm   loord

1   poooooooooooemmmmmm   mymymy   grooow

2   ẅẅ   ẅẅẅẅ   ah

3   zuhzuhzuhzuhzuh   lllllll   ṗ ṗ

69

1   ẇ   ẇ   wrtplrtplrtplrtplrtplrtplrtpl   pl pl

2   ah   ah   ha ha ha ha ha ha   heeeeeeeeee

3   Ṗ   Ṗ   MMMMMMMRRRRRRRRRRRR

1   eeeeeee pp leeeeeeeeeee

2   d   d   d   d   d   d d pdpdpdpd

3   zzz zzzzzzz mmmmmmmmmmmmmmmmmb

1   poet poet qwpt   qwpt   qwpt

2   dfll   dfll   dfll

3   b   b   vbvb   vbvb   vbvb

1   qwptqwptqwptqwptqwptqwptqwptqwpt

2   dflldflldflldflldflldflldflldfll

3   vbvbvbvbvbvbvbvbvbvbvbvb

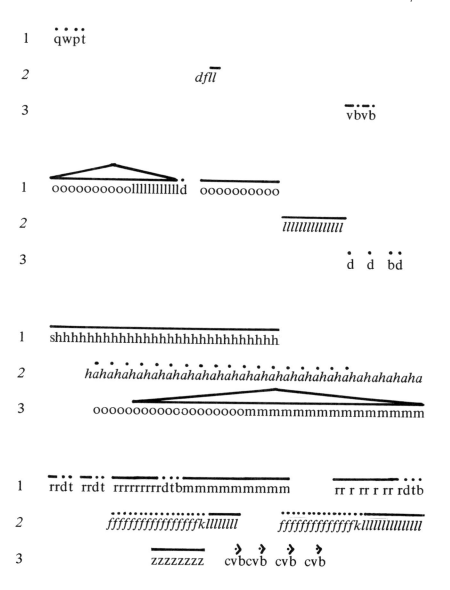

1   mmmmmmmmmmmmmmmmmmmmmmmmmmmmm

2   ṗ   ṗ   ṗ   ṗ   *raaaaaaaay*

3   zzzzzzzzzz   sssseeeeeee

1   ooooo   oooooo   oooooo   ṫ

2   *pray*   *pray*   *pray*   *ḋ*

3   ssseeeee   sssseeeeeeeeeeeeeeeemmmmmmmm   v̈b

1   ẗp   rfjkepooookjkjkjkjgkjkjkjgkjkjkjgkjkjkjg

2   *ḋf*   *lldf*   *lllldf*   *lllldfpdfpdfpppp*

3   v̈bw   eeioeeiouuuuuuiouiouiouiouiouiou

1   oooooooommmmmmoooooooooommmmmmmoooooooooo

2   *pray*   *pray*   *pray*   *pray*

3   peeaaccee   peeaaccee   peeaaccee

1   mmmmmmmooooooommmmm

2   *prayaaayyy*

3   peeaaccee   peeaacceee.

SOUND–COLOR SONATA

1 rrrrrrrrrrrrd rrrrrrrrrrrd w w w rrrrrrrrd rrrrrrrrd w w w

1 enw enw oooooooooooooollllll dd ddd dddd
2   rrrrrrrrrrd   w   w   w

1 oooooooooooooooollllll dd   pw pw   pdp
2   rrrrrrrrrrd w w w w   w w w

1 pdp mmmmmmmmmmmm rrrrrrrrd mmmmmmmmrrrrrrrrrrrrrr
2   w   w   w   w   bbooollllld

1 drrrrrrrrrr oh   oh   oh   oh pen   oh   pen
2 bbooollllld ah   ah   ah   ah   p   p p

1 zzzzkv zzzzkv kv kv kv kvdrrrrrrrrr
2 llllleeeeeeeeeeeeeeeeeeeed   d   d   d z z z

74

1   rrraaaaaaaaaaaaaaaaaaj   j   jooooooooooooook

2   *llllld*   *llllld*   *d*   *z*   *v*   *v*   *v*   *v*   *v*

1   ssssssssssssststststststststttttsssssss   ppppttttppppttttppppptttt

2   *peek*   *iiil*   *iiilll*

1   pp tt p t

2   oooooooooooooooooooooooooooooooooooooooo

1   ppt ppt ppt t ttp ttp ttp ttp p rrrrrdptdpt rrrrrrdptdpt

1   eeeeeeeeeegggooooo eeeeeeeeeeegggooooo goo gooo goooo

1   gooddooggoooddoooog googggd gahd dog

1   offffffffffffffttttfftttfftttfftttfftttfftttfffttbtbtbtbtb

1 shhhhhhhhhhhhhhhhhhhhhhhhhhhhhhhhhhhhhhhhhhhhhhhhh

2 *zzb* *zzb* *zzb* *zb* *zb* *zb* *zb*

1 hhhhhhhhhhhhhhhhhhhhhhhhhhhhh

2 *ppoppippoppippoppippopprrrdrrrd*

1 rrrrdrrrrdww   rrrrdrrrrdww   rrrrdrrrrdww

2   *eeep*   *eeep*   *eeepp w*

1 *llkj*   *llkj*   *fdaaaaah*   *wrrrk*   *fdaaaah*

2 *zzb*   *z zb zzb*   *p p*   *uppppp*

1 znmnz   znamna   znamnananananaooooooooooooo

2   *vv*   *kkk*   *dgkkdgkkdgkkdgkkdg*   *kk*

1 manaooooooooooooo   ooooh   ooooh   ooooh   ooooh

2   *pttt*   *pttt*   *pttt*   *pttt*   *p*

1   aaaah   aaaah   aaaah   aaaah

2   *ttt*   *ttt tt*   *t ttt t*   *t tt ttt tttt*   *t*   *t*

1   hmmmmmmmmmmmmmmmm   whyyyyyyyyyyyyyyyyyyyy

2   *v*   *v*   *v*   *bbee be   be*   *why*

1   yyyyyyyyyyy yes   wheeeeeeeeeeeeeeeeeeeeeeeeeeeee

2   *be*   *be why*   *bewhobewhy*   *dt*

1   eennnnnnnooooooowwwwww   rrrrrrrrrrd   rrrrrrrrrrd

2   *dt*   *dt*   *dtttttdd*   *t*   *w*   *w*

1   huuuuuuuuuuuuuuuuuu eblebeaaaaaaaaheeeeeeeeee

2   *zzbmmmmmzzb*   *why*   *not*

1   stststst   aahhp   opipopip

2   *why*   *oooh*   *b* *b* *b* *b*

1   rrrrrrrrrrr rrrrrrrrrr rrrrrrrrrr rrrrrrrrrr rrrrrrrrrr

2   *d*   *w*   *d*   *w*   *d*

ASSEMBLAGES

ASSEMBLAGE

1 My fingers   mingled
2   *Tears*   *winter moon*
3 Enlightened

1 with raindrops   and moonlight.
2   *madness*
3   is stillness.

1   Time flows
2   *everything.*
3 Contemplate   in mountain

1   shadows shudder
2 *And in moonlight*
3   springwater.

1 winter in the plum.
2   *plum-mingled snow*
3   Green creek

1   Weeping
2 *raindrops*   *and temple*
3   white moonlight.

1   wind
2   *from holy echoing.*
3 This is the cold   world void.

1   children's voices
2 *Children's voices*   *the sunbaked surf*
3

80

1
2
3

echoing madness

The clear knowledge   the spirit

1
2
3

shudders in flow   *from weeping*
          is silent of itself.

1
2
3

from the holy flute.

PURE PICKINGS

```
1              dusk                        dinner
2                    seen
3    Just tender                   I unused
4                        to me


1                        butterfly        or sit
2    receded revealing
3                    smog
4                              show


1
2                                   The flat clean
3    yearning to
4                believe the impossible.


1    draped
2
3         from it          Decided,
4               miracle.           said can't


1              out
2    and washed              Your
3                   and young.        hills
4                                   saw I


1    in a canvas                        three
2                   Staying observing
3                                   two
4               miracle.


1                                      after
2    broad belly        Gentle sunset
3                            ran past
4          like I.
```

```
1                                              like        big
2                    Season                        flat
3                              dropped back
4      I'd seen me.


1                          on trees
2                                  it rained.
3                By then                    Bodies pass
4      a never.


1                    surrounded before        just
2                                    hills        yesterday.
3
4      you opened


1                        by our
2                              clean ocean.
3            a twin
4      I asked                          My eyes


1                              or during
2                    as you are
3      girls by beach
4                                        to I.
```

TWO SHORT DADA CONVERSATIONS

I

```
1   On passing                    on meditation
2            bodies
3                       within
4                          mist


1                        Beach
2   exalts                      wondering
3          balance
4                  of spring.


1                          weeping
2                                radiant
3   precocious
4            settling sea                the silent


1   spring
2                                within
3          and final.    wondering
4                 Holy


1   the sun.                     daughter.
2          Tangled
3                       radiant
4                 beach              Silent


1          moments
2   tender
3                       melancholy.
4                 passing          Incline
```

84

1   from mist
2   *balance*
3   on daughter.
4   *on meditation*

1   on settling
2   *Perhaps*
3   tender   bodies
4   *at sun*

1   at sea
2   *and melancholy.*
3
4

II

1   Meditation
2   *balance*
3   from   the spring
4   *within*

1   on settling sea.
2   *and radiant*   *Perhaps*
3
4   *balance*

1   weeping
2   *Tender*
3   at beach   mist
4   *melancholy.*   *exalts*

```
1   daughter.
2                                    within melancholy
3
4              Incline bodies


1              passing sun.        mist              on
2                        Tangled
3   Mist on                              settling
4


1                   beach.
2                        Exalt
3                                      meditation
4   precocious              radiant


1              of spring.
2                                            silent
3   moments                    sea of sun
4                        And tender


1                             at the final
2              bodies
3   on passing                              weeping
4                        perhaps


1   moments
2
3              daughter
4                   wondering.
```

HAIKU

```
1                                    Mingled seaweed
2
3                        Holy beach
4       Drifting mountain


1                        raindrops
2       Our April                              with shadows
3                tears
4                          idly scribble


1                                    summer
2                    weeping
3       from the moon                          surf shudders
4                          poems


1                            surf and sun
2       tears              from
3
4          taking whatever              echoing night


1                            baked walls
2                    in willow
3            shadows
4       I like                          tangled cliff


1   childrens voices
2                    petals from our plum
3                                    everything
4


1
2
3   mingled
4           A cold mind.
```

RANDOM SELECTIONS

1 Nothing ever dies
2   *As labor progresses*
3   Once this decision

1 from the outside.
2   *and the contractions*
3   has been made

1   No one can kill
2 *come more quickly*
3   Chambers began

1 your character.   No one can kill
2   *and become stronger*
3   to work out

1   your peace of mind.
2 *the woman*
3   the order of his going.

1   No one can kill
2 *should assume*
3   Too deeply involved

1   your business
2 *the left lateral position*
3   not to menace

1   or your reputation
2 *for relaxation*
3   the entire apparatus.

1   or anything
2   *as described earlier.*
3   "This is a very serious matter"

1   that is yours.
2   *The supine position*   *interferes*
3   he said.

1   You can
2   *with adequate circulation.*
3   He had gained

1   but nobody else can.
2   *Before assuming*
3   that hard experience

1
2   *this position*   *she should make certain*
3   in the desperate days.

1   No man or woman
2   *that her bladder*
3   He knew   once more

1
2   *is empty.*   *All her joints*
3   what his boyhood confusions

1   was ever yet destroyed   from the outside.
2
3   had vaguely uttered.

1   Remind yourself constantly
2   *every one*   *must be loose*
3

1   write it down   where you will see
2   *and bent slightly*
3   After this

1   it often.   Have it on
2   *her knee and upper thigh*
3   you and I.

1   your desk.   Hang it in your
2   *firmly supported.*
3   It costs so little.

1   bedroom.
2   *Following the birth*
3   Among potting composts

1   Write it in your pocketbook.
2   *the husband has new responsibilities*
3

1   Write it on
2   *not only in relation to his wife*
3   for adult plants

1   your soul.   It will
2   *but to his new born.*
3   the most favored

1   transform your life.
2
3   to become dry periodically is good.

1   It will bring you to God.

ZEN DROPPINGS

1 Where   has the country gone?
2   *I picked up*
3   You laughed

1   Now fading
2   *our love.*   *I gave you*
3 but within   the heart

1   in sorrow.
2 *red snow.*
3   was sore   and windy.

1 Where is Spring?   Spring is falling.
2   *Let it fall*
3

1   Where is youth?
2   *into the moment.*
3 Laughter looked

1   Youth
2   *Dust upon*
3 cruel mocking   at the wild jest.

1   is in sadness.
2 *the tulip.*
3   The sore heart was you.

1 Sorrow has numbered flowers.
2   *Let it in.*
3

PATTERNS

```
1      Care and you
2                              towering
3                     arises
4      Over                                  class


1            patterns
2      hidden          look
3                          and part
4                          still itself


1      comfortable                          supports
2                  the cul-de-sac
3
4                          rather more


1                    or folds
2                          Garden of Eden
3      when in position
4                                  becomes as


1      white                  it, and
2                  anxious
3            half-tone
4                          worships want


1                  the
2                  older walk
3      especially with
4                          not its back stuff


1      separates we
2            living we
3                              taken
4                  and illusion        begin it
```

```
1              soft you
2    a valley              heaven freshness
3                                        a regard of one
4


1
2                    ocean found
3
4    obvious why                              a mode for
                          and own and more


1              softly
2                              but nice on trees
3    the whole
4                    go familar


1                              great          see
2
3                    and is part
4    less than vulgar              and again


1                                        why not
2        for another    is dewy    easy
3                              the steps
4                          more


1                              about how cool.
2                    quiet and what
3              in
4    but enjoys
```

THEME AND VARIATIONS

I

1   There are no dirty words
2   *just very dirty minds*

1   are no dirty words there
2   *very dirty minds just*

1   no dirty words there are
2   *dirty minds just very*

1   dirty words there are no
2   *minds just very dirty*

1   words there are no dirty
2   *just very dirty minds*

II

1   are there no dirty
2   *just very minds*

1   words know there are
2   *dirty just minds*

1   dirty dirty words are
2   *very minds just*

1   no dirty words are
2   *very very just*

94

III

1 there are no
2
                             dirty minds

1 words are dirty
2
                             very just

1 no words are
2
                             dirty minds

IV

1 are dirty
2
                                 minds

1 no words
2
                                   dirty

V

1 words
2
                                   minds

PARTING

1 And a final brief moment of language
2   *And a final brief*
3

1 words laced together   in joy
2   *moment*
3   And a final

1   of being
2 *of language*   *words*
3   brief moment   of language

1 in sadness   of parting.
2   *laced together*   *in joy*
3   words

1   We have worked   together.
2   *of being*
3 laced together

1   We have invented   poems
2   *in sadness*
3 in joy   of being

1   together.
2 *of parting.*   *We have worked*
3   in sadness

1 Our voices   have touched
2   *together.*
3   of parting.

96

1   felt.
2   *We have invented*   *poems*
3   We have worked   together.

1   And perhaps   for this reason
2
3   We have   invented poems

1   it will be
2   *together.*   *Our voices*
3   together.

1   easier for us to
2   *have touched*
3   Our voices have

1   come together   in another place
2   *felt.*   *And perhaps*
3   touched

1
2   *for this reason*   *it will be easier*
3   felt.   And perhaps

1   in another time.
2   *for us to come together*
3

1
2   *in another place*   *in another time.*
3   for this reason it will be easier

3   for us to come together in another place in another time.

Cover design by Marek A. Majewski